ALL ACCESS
DEMI LOVATO

By Riley Brooks

SCHOLASTIC INC.

New York   Toronto   London   Auckland   Sydney
Mexico City   New Delhi   Hong Kong   Buenos Aires

© 2009 by Scholastic

ISBN-13: 978-0-545-17592-0
ISBN-10: 0-545-17592-5

Published by Scholastic Inc.
SCHOLASTIC and associated logos are trademarks and/or registered trademarks of Scholastic Inc.

12 11 10 9 8 7 6 5 4 3 2   9 10 11 12 13 14/0

Designed by Deena Fleming
Printed in the U.S.A.
First printing, June 2009

CONTENTS:

Introduction: Hello, Red Carpet!   1

Chapter 1: Texas Sweetheart   7

Chapter 2: Demi's Dreams   17

Chapter 3: Mean Girls   27

Chapter 4: Demi's Return   41

Chapter 5: This Is Me   47

Chapter 6: Just the Jonas Brothers   59

Chapter 7: Don't Forget   71

Chapter 8: True Princesses   84

Chapter 9: Demi Takes a Chance   93

Chapter 10: Behind the Scenes   102

Chapter 11: Demi's Future   119

Chapter 12: Quiz: How Well Do You Know Demi?   124

Chapter 13: Just the Facts   134

Chapter 14: Demi Online   137

CONTENTS

INTRODUCTION:
Hello, Red Carpet!

The evening of November 23, 2008, was a beautiful night in the sparkling city of Los Angeles as the biggest and brightest stars in the music business lit up the red carpet at the Nokia Theatre for the American Music Awards. But before the stars could make their way into the theater, they had to walk down the red carpet, stopping to pose for photographs and to give interviews.

ABC's Chris Harrison was one of the celebrity interviewers that night and he must have been pretty psyched. After all, he was getting to chat with all of the biggest stars! He spoke with everyone from the Pussycat

Dolls to the 2008 *Project Runway* winner, Christian Siriano. But one of the most exciting people on his must-interview list was the girl who would introduce the Jonas Brothers that night — up-and-coming teen star and Disney darling Demi Lovato.

Chris Harrison had certainly done his homework. Demi had just dropped her first album and had starred in the hit Disney television movie *Camp Rock* that summer. That night, she looked absolutely stunning in her white Gustavo Cadile dress with a black sash around her waist. Her gorgeous chocolate-brown hair was pulled off her face in a partial updo. Demi looked like she had been born to walk the red carpet. Smiling and confident, Demi stood next to Chris as he began the interview.

"Amazingly enough," Chris Harrison started, "you're sixteen years old and you wrote most of your songs. You're sixteen, where does your inspiration come from?"

It took Demi less than a second to respond. "Believe it or not, being sixteen, I've been through a lot," she replied.

"Come on, how much heartbreak can you have at sixteen?" Chris continued.

"A lot," Demi said, laughing. "No, you've gotta make the best of it and so that's what I've learned to do. And I actually spend a lot of time in my room writing rather than going out and hanging out with people, which is kind of embarrassing, but . . ." She trailed off, waiting for the next question. But Demi shouldn't have been embarrassed. All she had admitted was that she took her career seriously and that she would rather work on her music than go out and party like many other young celebrities.

Demi must have breathed a sigh of relief after she finished her interview with Chris. It had been her first interview of the night and she had passed the test. But she knew the true test of her star quality that night would come when she introduced the Jonas Brothers.

It was an incredible awards show for Demi. There were performances from some huge names like Christina Aguilera, Pink, Taylor Swift, Miley Cyrus, and Beyoncé. And Demi even got to meet one of her music idols, the heavy metal band Mötley Crüe! But Demi was especially excited for another reason. She was waiting in the back wings of the Nokia Theatre to introduce the hottest teen band in the country, the Jonas Brothers. She had opened up for the Jonas Brothers on their summer 2008 tour, but this was different. Demi wouldn't be belting out a song she wrote in an arena packed with cheering fans who were there just to see her and the Jonas Brothers. This time, Demi would be speaking in front of some of the most respected musicians in the world, not to mention the entire audience of over 12 million people watching from their couches at home!

Demi was probably pretty nervous, but she didn't let it show. When it was finally time for her to take the stage, she took a deep breath and stood in front of the microphone. She flashed her adorable smile and began, "I had the best time making this movie this year called *Camp Rock* and working with three great guys who acted in the film with me. I guess they sing a little too, and they all have the same last name. Coincidence? You be the judge. Please give a great welcome to three of my best friends. Singing a hit from their album *A Little Bit Longer*, here are the Jonas Brothers!"

The crowd roared with applause. Demi quickly walked toward the back of the stage as the lights switched their focus from her to Nick, Kevin, and Joe Jonas. They performed their hit "Tonight" to thunderous applause and screaming fans. Later that night they would go on to win the T-Mobile Breakthrough Artist Award. Demi must have been proud of her three friends, and honored to have had the chance to share the night with them. After all, she really couldn't have asked for a better way to make her debut in the professional music community than by introducing such a sensational band! And with Demi's talent and drive to succeed, it certainly won't be long before she's winning awards herself!

CHAPTER 1:
Texas Sweetheart

When Diana and Patrick Lovato found out that they would be welcoming a second beautiful baby girl into their home, they had no idea that she would be famous at the age of 16! It was a typical hot and sunny summer day in Dallas, Texas, on August 20, 1992, when Demetria Devonne Lovato entered the world. Demi was a beautiful, healthy baby girl with big brown eyes and an adorable smile. Her parents couldn't have been more excited to celebrate her arrival, and Demi instantly joined her older sister, Dallas, as the light of her parents' lives!

Right from the start, Demi's parents wanted to give their daughter a strong, unique name. They decided on Demetria. That's right, Demi is short for Demetria! Demetria is a name that comes from the Greek word that means "earth mother" and "goddess of fertility." Her middle name, Devonne, is of English origin, and it means "divine." Although the name is certainly beautiful, Demetria *is* a bit of a mouthful, and very difficult for a little girl to learn how to pronounce and spell. So, Diana and Patrick shortened Demetria's name to Demi, a nickname that has stuck with her to this day.

Demi grew up in Colleyville, which is a friendly suburb of Dallas, Texas. Demi was in good company growing up in the Lone Star State, since a lot of other fantastic actors are from there too! Jennifer Garner from *13 Going on 30*, Haylie Duff (Hilary Duff's big sis), Alexis Bledel from *The Sisterhood of the Traveling Pants* and *Gilmore Girls*, Jennifer Love Hewitt, Matthew McConaughey, and brothers Owen and Luke Wilson are all from Texas. Demi's best friend, Selena Gomez, also shares her home state with Demi. As they say, "Everything is bigger in Texas" — even the stars!

In the early 1980s Demi's mother, Diana Hart, was a professional cheerleader for the National Football League team the Dallas Cowboys. The Dallas Cowboys Cheerleaders are world famous for being the most beautiful, talented, and entertaining cheerleaders around, and making the squad is very, very difficult. Diana had to undergo strenuous auditions for days before making the cut. But it was all worth it to her because Diana loved cheerleading. She was a great dancer with tons of energy, and she absolutely adored performing in front of the huge crowds every week. After she retired from professional cheerleading, Diana decided to pursue a singing career. She wasn't ready to give up performing and she had a beautiful voice, so it was a perfect fit!

Diana worked very hard to get her foot in the door.

The music industry is notoriously difficult to break into, but Diana was determined and she eventually became a country music recording artist. Demi proudly told *Entertainment Weekly* that her mother ". . . opened at Six Flags for, like, Reba McEntire and George Strait." Musical talent and stage presence certainly run in the Lovato family!

Demi took after her mother in a lot of ways. As a child, Demi had a lot of energy and was always smiling. She also loved being the center of attention, as Demi's dad, Patrick, told *Star* magazine, "Demi loved being on the go and hated to sit still." The Lovato household was perfect for such an energetic little girl. There was always a lot going on and it usually involved music. Patrick was in a band when he was younger and Demi's mom was pursuing her country music career when Demi was little. "I would sit baby Demi on my lap and play guitar to her. She'd look up at me and smile," Patrick told *Star* magazine.

Demi wasn't the only little Lovato who loved music. Demi's big sister, Dallas, has a lot of musical talent as well. Dallas was four years old when Demi was born, and she must have been so excited to finally have a little sister to play with! The girls are as close as sisters can be, and Demi has always looked up to her older sister. Demi and Dallas are both natural performers and they loved to ham it up, putting on shows and skits for their parents. They both also inherited beautiful voices from their mother, and they loved to sing. Dallas told *Portrait* magazine, "I started having a love for music when I was about three. . . . My first memories are being in the tour bus and watching my mom light up the stage. I knew then that I wanted to follow in her footsteps and pursue a music career as well." Demi and Dallas each have a unique look because of their Irish, Italian, and Hispanic heritage. Dallas has chestnut-colored hair that she sometimes highlights with blond streaks, and big brown eyes that look a lot like Demi's!

Demi's early childhood was full of happy moments, but 1994 turned out to be a very tough year for the entire Lovato family. Demi's parents had not been getting along very well for a long time. Even though they tried really hard to make their relationship work, Patrick and Diana eventually decided that they had to separate. Patrick told *Star* magazine that as much as he loved Diana, they just wanted different things: "I was working fourteen hours at my contracting business, and she was still touring. The breakup was inevitable, but I loved her then, and I still do. She's been a great mother to our children." Patrick and Diana have remained friendly, but the divorce still wasn't fun for anyone, even if it was the best course for the family to take in the long run. Demi was only a toddler when her parents' divorce was finalized, so she probably didn't completely understand what was happening at the time. Luckily, her parents made it very clear that they both loved her very much and would always be there for her, no matter what.

After the divorce, Demi and Dallas lived with their mom in Texas while their dad moved to New Mexico to be closer to Demi's grandpa Frank. Both girls wished their father was closer, especially since the distance made it difficult to stay in touch. Patrick was diagnosed with cancer, which made it difficult for him to travel. At the time, Dallas and Demi were too little to fly alone to visit their father. Plus, money was pretty tight and long trips are expensive. Patrick fought the cancer, but it was a long, hard struggle that didn't leave much time for being a father. He's a survivor today, which has definitely inspired Demi. If her dad could fight and win against cancer, then she could do anything she set her mind to! According to *Star* magazine, they once went four whole years without seeing each other. Demi talked to her dad on the phone occasionally, but he wasn't able to be a very big part of her life from so far away. Luckily for Demi, it wasn't long before there was another father figure in her life!

Shortly after Patrick moved to New Mexico, Demi's mother fell in love with a man named Eddie DeLaGarza. Eddie is kind, family-focused, and an excellent father figure. He's very athletic and he used to play football and baseball in high school and in college at Texas Tech University. Diana instantly fell in love with his gentleness, his devotion to family, and his adoration for Diana and her girls. Demi and Dallas thought Eddie was great, so they were probably pretty psyched when he and Diana were married. Eddie loved being a dad to Demi and Dallas and he has been wholly devoted to his stepdaughters ever since. And they have been devoted to him too. Both girls call Eddie "Dad" and they really do think of him as their father, especially since their real father was never around when they were growing up.

With the support of their mom and stepfather, the Lovato girls grew into accomplished and talented young ladies who made their parents very proud. But the family wasn't complete yet. In 2001, when Demi was ten years old, she found out that Eddie and her mother were going to have a baby! Demi must have been so excited. She'd always wanted a little sister so she wouldn't be the youngest anymore. On December 28, 2001, Demi's little sister, Madison, was born. Madison was the best Christmas gift Demi's family could have asked for. She was so cute that Demi didn't even mind helping out with the ickier stuff like changing diapers! Despite the big age difference between the two oldest girls and Madison, all three sisters get along really well. In fact, Demi told *Scholastic News* that one of her favorite childhood memories is "driving around in the hot Texas sun, singing while driving with the windows down. My sister Madison and I are always together. I can't pick one moment. I love being with her . . . she's so much fun and so funny. I am always quoting her. [And my sister] Dallas — both are very caring and honest. I know that I can always ask them anything and they will give me their best opinion." Madison definitely looks up to her older sisters and they try to spend as much time with her as they can, no matter how busy they are.

Demi's parents are devoted to making sure their three daughters have the best in life and that they all accomplish their dreams. Dallas, Demi, and Madison are so lucky to have parents who are so dedicated to making their dreams come true. And they're even more lucky to have one another!

CHAPTER 2:
Demi's Dreams

Demi knew from a very young age that she loved the spotlight, but it was Demi's mom who really inspired her to pursue a career in singing. Demi told tvguide.com that her mother "brought the singing out of me. She was a singer and she went on tour with big names, so I . . . was born hearing her sing. You know, I would hear singing in the shower . . . and I was like, 'I want to sing!' So in kindergarten one day, I decided that I wanted to do the talent show. So I started listening to a song that I really wanted to do and basically, ever since then, I started singing." It must have been great for Demi to have a successful role model right there at home. Her mom encouraged her, coached her, and reminded Demi every day that she could achieve her dreams.

It's not that often that a kindergartner knows what they want to be when they grow up. Many little girls hope to be a princess, a ballerina, or a mermaid when they get older. But Demi wasn't one of them. She has known that her place was in the spotlight since her kindergarten talent show. Demi had chosen to sing Celine Dion's "My Heart Will Go On," a very difficult song with lots of high notes. The song was the theme song for *Titanic*, a blockbuster movie that had come out that year starring Kate Winslet and Leonardo DiCaprio. Demi loved singing the song at home, but she got really nervous when she had to sing it in front of her class. "I was on stage, and I actually messed up, but then it started going again, so it was good," Demi told the *Dallas Observer*. "I just kept it up. And at that moment, when I stuck through it and stopped crying onstage, I guess that's when I realized, 'Wow, I don't hate this enough to run offstage.' . . . I always knew that one day, somehow, I'd be here where I am today. Or at least, I was dreaming it." It must have taken a lot of courage for little Demi to stick it out and keep singing even after messing up! All of the parents were impressed, especially Demi's stepfather, who was in the audience cheering her on. "That's a hard song to sing for anyone, much less a five-year-old," he told the *Houston Press* in 2008. Demi knew that the show must go on and so she stuck it out. She was a pro even then!

Of course, landing her dream career wasn't easy. It took years and years of hard work and devotion. "We just searched for routes and ways to make it, and that's what it really takes. You're not always presented with the opportunities, but we went out and we searched for it," Demi explained to the *Dallas Observer.* Demi had grown up tagging along with her big sis, Dallas, to her dance and vocal lessons and auditions, so Demi knew it would be tough, but she didn't let that stop her. Demi and her mom and stepdad went to every audition in the area. She tried out for commercials, plays, voice-over work, movies, and television shows. It must have been grueling to go to all of those auditions, especially since Demi heard "no" a lot, but she didn't give up. She was always searching for more opportunities, and she also took voice, dance, and acting lessons to hone her skills.

When traditional avenues didn't pan out, Demi tried other things. She competed in beauty pageants, and even tried her hand at some modeling. She figured that every experience helped her performing skills, no matter how unrelated it seemed at the time. Demi especially loved entering pageants. In an interview with Kidd Kraddick, she said, "Pageants mean a lot to me." Deep down, Demi is a pageant girl, which is a tradition many Texan families are a part of. She told Kidd

Kraddick, "I competed in a lot, but I won a few." One of the competitions she won was the Texas Cinderella State Mini Miss 2000 pageant, when she was nine. Demi's impressive interviewing skills, natural charm, and amazing voice always wowed the judges.

When Demi was just six years old, she got a really big break. She went to an open audition for *Barney & Friends,* a popular television show for preschoolers. *Barney & Friends* was a very well-known show about a singing purple dinosaur named Barney and his friends at an elementary school. The show featured a cast of adorable kids of different ages who could sing, dance, and act along with Barney. When several of the cast members became too old to continue on the show, producers would hold open auditions to replace them with fresh new talent. Demi was probably pretty psyched about the audition. It was a preschool show, but it was so popular that landing the part would guarantee national recognition.

Demi wasn't the only one who wanted a part. Over 1,400 girls showed up to the casting call for the show in Dallas. While standing in line, Demi was kind of bored and nervous so she invited another girl in line to sit and color with her. Even though they were up for the same part, Demi and her new friend hit it off instantly. When they got to the front of the line and went their separate ways into the audition rooms, the girls wished each other the best of luck. What the two didn't know was that they had just formed a friendship that would last a lifetime. Demi had just met her BFF, Selena Gomez.

Competing against 1,400 other kids for a role is some serious competition, so Diana wasn't overly confident that Demi would be hearing back from the Barney executives. Even when Demi got a callback, Diana still was not confident that Demi would book the job. After all, the second round of auditions still included hundreds of girls and it was being held at the same time as an annual beauty pageant in Las Vegas that Dallas and Demi loved going to. Diana told the *Dallas Observer,* "I said, 'You know, I don't know about this.' I was like, 'We audition for stuff all the time, and we haven't really gotten anything. I'm just not sure that I want her to miss that week of fun that she looks forward to every year, all year.' And they said, 'We really, really want to see her here.'" The casting director loved Demi so much that Diana decided to ask Demi what she wanted to do. Diana trusted Demi to make the right choice for herself. "I told her, 'You know what the chances are. You know this business that we've been in so far. If you really would like to do the acting career and the singing and the dancing that goes along with it, you're going to need to stay behind with your aunt while we go. If you don't want to do that, and you want to go have your fun for the week, I totally understand that. I'm going to leave it up to you.' She thought about it for three seconds and said, 'I need to stay here,'"

Dianna told the *Dallas Observer*. Even then, Demi knew that she needed to make sacrifices in order to pursue her dream. Since Dallas looked forward to the pageant every year, Diana still took her to Las Vegas while Demi stayed with her aunt in Texas.

In the end, Demi's insistence on attending the second round of *Barney* auditions paid off. Demi booked her first television gig as Angela on *Barney & Friends* during that callback. Demi didn't let the pressure that comes with trying out as one of 1,400 potential Angelas get to her. When she learned that she was the one the casting directors picked out of all of those other talented girls, Demi felt amazing!

One of those talented girls turned out to be Demi's coloring buddy, Selena! Selena's character on *Barney* was named Gianna. Selena was starting her television career on *Barney & Friends*, just like Demi. The two would film *Barney & Friends* together for two seasons. Little did the two girls know that one day they would have their own television shows on Disney where they would be the stars!

Barney & Friends was an international sensation, so having her name and face on such a big show was very important for Demi's career. *Barney & Friends* aired on PBS in the United States and was shown in thirteen other countries, including Japan, Israel, Spain, and Mexico. The show was even nominated for seven Daytime Emmy awards from 1994 to 2008, with one win in 2001 for sound mixing.

Demi's character, Angela, was smart and *soo* cute. In one 2002 episode, Angela was a singing crossing guard. Her song was about teaching kids to look both ways and to pay attention to stoplights before crossing the street. Even when she was a little girl, Demi was an excellent role model!

Working on *Barney* was a lot of fun and Demi had a great time with her cast mates, but it was also an incredible learning experience. A regular role on a television show meant learning lines, songs, and choreography every week, plus seeing what goes on behind the scenes. It was a great way for Demi to learn about the responsibilities of being a working actor, and she still uses what she learned on *Barney & Friends* today!

CHAPTER 3:
Mean Girls

A lot of great things came from Demi's run on *Barney* — she had started her television career and met her best friend, Selena. But sadly, her success also led to jealousy from her peers, especially when she got to middle school. Demi had always had plenty of friends growing up and she was friendly, happy, and fun to be around. So you would think she would have been popular — especially since she was an actress! Unfortunately, the opposite was true.

During elementary school, Demi loved everything about school, especially recess. Demi told *J-14*, "I wasn't shy. I was very outgoing. I'm pretty much the same person as I am now, but I didn't know who I was." In fifth grade, Demi even had one of the coolest lockers as she explained to *J-14*, "It had a mirror so I could check my makeup — every girl had one! I had pictures of my friends and me." Some of her friends were a little jealous of her success and teased her for being on *Barney*. But Demi knew how to handle it, and she thought she was ready for the transition to middle school.

In 2003, Demi tried to focus a little more on music even though she was still going on auditions for film projects. She had finished filming *Barney & Friends* and was ready for a new challenge. So, with her singing career in mind, Demi put out her first music video when she was only 11 years old! Demi's first music video featured a song she sang called "Moves Me." The music video featured a young, cute Demi dancing in a pink shirt and black pants. She had a microphone hooked onto her ear, and half of her hair was pulled back away from her face. Demi even had backup dancers! That's right, the video also has two boys and two girls as backup dancers. All of the performers, including Demi, are wearing one black wristband. Her video was featured on a hip-hop dance video put out by Fenton "F-Troop" Fulgham, a well-known choreographer. The dance video was called "Off Da Hook F-Troop Style" and it taught kids how to do all of Fenton's awesome dances. Demi loved his choreography, which made it even cooler to have her music video affiliated with him.

When Demi began attending Cross Timbers Middle School, she was really excited! Her singing and acting career seemed to be working out and she was happy to see all her friends. But soon she felt uncomfortable going to school. There was a crowd of popular girls at school that had decided to make Demi's life miserable.

Instead of playfully teasing her for being on *Barney*, they bullied her constantly, as she explained to *Entertainment Weekly*: "I had a hate wall in the bathroom, and everyone signed a petition that said 'We all hate Demi Lovato.'" Demi wasn't the only one who was scared of the mean girls. Everyone else was just as afraid of them, which meant that no one was willing to be friends with Demi or to stand up for her. It must have been awful to have to go to school and face those mean students every day, especially with no other friends to cheer her up.

At first, Demi couldn't figure out what it was about her that made the mean girls pick on her. But Demi hadn't done anything wrong. The truth was that Demi had something that those mean girls wanted — talent, determination, and success. Her classmates were so jealous of Demi's bright future that they tried to make her feel small. Luckily, Demi had her family and Selena to help her get through it.

After appearing on *Barney*, Selena had to deal with jealous students too. Selena told Discoverygirls.com, "I'd miss a couple of weeks for *Barney* and then I'd go back to school and I'd deal with some jealousy. I wouldn't talk about the show unless somebody said, 'How was your episode?' So not a lot of people were jealous — just this one group of girls who didn't like me." It was definitely nice for Selena and Demi to have each other to lean on when things were rough at school. And going through those experiences together only made their friendship stronger!

It was probably tempting for Demi to fight back against her bullies, but instead she decided to be the bigger person. She didn't make fun of those girls or spread rumors about them. Instead she turned to her music as an outlet for all the pain and anger she felt. "Everybody has an enemy, the girl who just doesn't look like you," Demi told *Teen* magazine. "I never really got to do anything back [to those girls] until I wrote a song about it." Writing songs about everything she was going through really helped Demi get through the hard days. "When I was in school, all I held on to was music. When kids are dealing with bullying, they should have something to hold on to. When you focus on better things, it pays off. Those girls are still bullying people, but I'm doing better things," Demi explained to *Tiger Beat*.

Eventually, Demi and her parents decided homeschooling would be much better for her. She had done everything she could to try to handle the bullying herself, but it was really affecting her self-esteem and her schoolwork. So Demi opted out of traditional schooling in seventh grade and began to meet with tutors instead. While she probably missed some things about going to class with other kids her age, like going to dances and meeting new friends, Demi definitely did not miss the mean girls! Plus, without those distractions, she was able to concentrate more on the most important thing about school — her studies. "When I started homeschooling, I tested two grades above where I should be," Demi explained to *J-14*.

Homeschooling was the ideal choice for Demi. She made great grades, had lots of extra time to work on her music and acting career, and was able to spend her downtime with her real friends. All of that time spent on her music really helped Demi find her voice and the unique sound that her fans love now. "Since I started homeschooling, I got more in touch with who I am and I realized rock is the way to go," Demi told *J-14*. Of course, homeschooling isn't for everyone, but it did work out well for Demi.

After Demi's run on seasons seven and eight of *Barney & Friends*, she went on a lot of auditions. Sometimes she and Selena would go to auditions together, which always made it more fun. The best friends helped each other get through the stress of auditions and the pain of rejection when they didn't book parts. They had a lot of fun giggling and singing along to the radio during long car rides, but occasionally the trips didn't go as smoothly as they would have liked. On the way to Austin, Texas, for a Disney talent search, Demi and Selena got into a very sticky situation. "On the way, we stopped for strawberry milk shakes and drank them in the car. When we were done, my older sister, Dallas, threw hers out the car window. My backseat window happened to be down, so the milk shake came into the car and splattered all over me and Selena! We had to wash our hair at a gas station on the way to the audition!" Demi dished to *Twist*. Luckily, both girls were talented enough to outshine any strawberry spatters!

There were times when it was difficult to be best friends with another actress — like when Selena booked roles and Demi didn't. Only a year after her final season on *Barney*, Selena won a small part in a really big movie. *Spy Kids 3-D: Game Over* was the third movie in the popular movie series *Spy Kids*. Selena joined big-name actors like Antonio Banderas, Sylvester Stallone, and Salma Hayek for the film. It must have been especially difficult for Demi to watch her best friend achieve success so quickly. After all, Selena had never auditioned for anything before *Barney*, but Demi had been auditioning since she was five years old. Both girls heard "no" a lot, but Selena had a little more success than Demi. They tried to support each other as much as they could. But it wasn't always easy for them to get together, especially when Selena was busy working.

After going on a lot of auditions but nothing really working out, Demi decided to take a break from acting. "After hundreds of auditions and nothing, you're sitting home and wondering, 'What am I doing?'" Demi explained to the *New York Daily News.* The school bullies certainly hadn't helped Demi's confidence. "I'd gone through so much rejection at that point with girls at school that I couldn't do acting anymore, where all I was doing was working hard and hearing 'no,'" Demi told the *Washington Post.* But performing has always been a big part of who Demi is and she couldn't stay away for long.

It must have taken a lot of courage to face being rejected at auditions *and* being rejected at school by her classmates. Demi told the *Washington Post,* "I started missing [acting], and once I got back into it, that's when things started rolling. I think that's because there was a new drive in it, there was more passion than there was before." But rejection happens once in a while to everyone, no matter how talented they are. At least Demi had the strength of mind to take a step back from her career and really think about what she wanted.

Demi switched to homeschooling around that time, which meant she was happier and more confident going into her auditions — and that couldn't have hurt! It took Demi just a few years to gather enough courage and get back into the groove of going to audition after audition. After all, facing rejection is difficult, even for someone as awesome as Demi! Taking a step away from her dreams just reminded Demi how important they were to her — and nothing, not even bullying, was going to stop her from rising to the top!

With new motivation, Demi began to really focus on exactly what she wanted to do with her career. She signed up for classes to help improve her natural talents and spent lots of time practicing. Demi took her singing lessons at Linda Septien's studio in Addison, Texas. Ms. Septien has a really good record of working with other successful singers. Some of her famous past students include Ryan Cabrera and sisters Jessica Simpson and Ashlee Simpson-Wentz, just to name a few. Ms. Septien is definitely no stranger to talent, and she instantly knew that Demi was special. Demi really applied herself to her lessons and rehearsed like crazy at home. Demi's skills grew quickly, and by the time Demi was 10 years old, she was already in the advanced class, wowing her teacher with R&B and pop songs.

Demi loved writing and singing her own music, but she also mastered the ability to put an amazing personal twist on other people's songs in her classes. As for Demi's star quality, Ms. Septien told the *Dallas Observer,* "There are just some kids who are born entertaining. They seek people to watch them, and they want to know so much." Demi was definitely one of those kids! Since Demi has always loved writing her own songs, she also took guitar and piano lessons. They definitely paid off, because these days Demi can play both of them like a pro! And she can also do a mean drum solo if given the chance.

But Demi wasn't satisfied with just singing and instrumental lessons, she wanted to be a triple threat — a performer who can sing, dance, and act. There aren't that many people in the world who are talented in every aspect of performing, but Demi was determined to be one of them. That's why Demi begged for acting lessons at EveryBody Fits studio in Coppell, Texas. Luckily, her mom gave in and signed Demi up. She took classes from Cathryn Sullivan, a very well-known acting coach in the area. Cathryn has a son who is just a little bit older than Demi. His name is Cody Linley and he took some classes with Demi. Cody's made several appearances on *Hannah Montana*. The two have remained close friends, especially since they both ended up in the Disney family. They have even dated — but more on that later!

Demi was working hard taking classes and going to auditions, but she wasn't in it alone. Her family and friends were right there with her, encouraging her and helping think of new ways to get Demi noticed. Diana and Eddie paid for and drove her to and from each lesson, and the whole time, they never stopped cheering on their daughter. With such a supportive family to back up her talents, how could Demi not succeed?

CHAPTER 4:
Demi's Return

Demi was back in the game. She was working her butt off at all of her classes and going to as many auditions as she could. Her renewed passion and dedication definitely paid off. She landed a role in a 2006 episode of the hit television program *Prison Break*. In the episode "First Down," Demi played Danielle Curtin, a girl whose father protects her from a bad guy. It was a relatively small role, but Demi has always known that any role is a good role. After all, Demi got her face and name out there on a highly viewed prime-time television show, which was a big deal. Landing the role also gave her the courage to keep auditioning for other, bigger acting gigs.

A year later, a Disney casting call led to Demi scoring a role on *As the Bell Rings*. *As the Bell Rings* was a mini-show that aired during commercial breaks on the Disney Channel in five-minute segments. It was filmed outside of Austin, right in Demi's home state of Texas! She wouldn't even have to move to L.A. to take the part. Demi told *Tiger Beat* how nervous she was before the audition: "I remember when I auditioned for *As the Bell Rings*, I walked into the audition thinking I wasn't going to get it. I was really serious about it and I broke down and cried. My acting coach was like, 'You can do it!' So when I went to the audition, I didn't get any feedback, the [casting directors] basically didn't look at me and I started tearing up. I was like, 'I didn't get it,' but then I booked it! I was so excited — it was so awesome!"

At first, Demi was nervous about accepting the role. She had never been in a comedy before, and she didn't think that she was funny enough. Demi told *Entertainment Weekly*, "When I got the part, I actually cried. I thought, I'm not going to be able to do this — I'm not funny! I'm never going to be able to work for the Disney Channel, because they're based on comedy." But Demi gathered her courage and went for it anyway. Once she got on set and was able to let go of her nerves, Demi proved that she could handle comedy, and made millions of viewers look forward to laughing along with Demi's character, Charlotte Adams.

Demi described her character Charlotte to *Blast* magazine: "She has a crush on Danny, and she has two best friends, Tiffany and Brooke, and she learns a lot from them." Demi's best friends were played by Carlson Young and Gabriella Rodriguez. Tony Oller played Danny and Seth Ginsberg played Toejam. Seth is from Texas, just like Demi!

Since episodes of *As the Bell Rings* were only five minutes long, the actors had to get laughs pretty quickly. Demi told *Blast* magazine, "It's awesome to do the show — very fast paced and fun!" In one funny episode of *As the Bell Rings*, titled "Flower Day," Danny, Charlotte's crush, debates whether or not he should send Charlotte a flower. If he gets one for her and she doesn't get one for him, he'll look totally lame. On the other hand, if she sends him a flower and he doesn't return the favor, he'll still look lame. His friends suggest pulling a "Flower Day flu," but he dismisses that option right off the bat.

In the next scene, Charlotte's two friends ask her if she is going to send Danny a flower. As Charlotte's nerdy friend discusses the silliness behind the idea of "Flower Day," Charlotte's other friend, a pretty blond, accepts flowers from almost every guy who passes the three girls. Charlotte's and Danny's friends eventually come up with a plan: The girls will tell Danny that Charlotte got him a flower, and the boys will tell Charlotte that Danny got her one. But by the time Danny makes up his mind and tries to buy Charlotte a flower, they're all sold out! The same thing happens to Charlotte. So Charlotte gets Danny a backup flower, a huge red-and-orange one made out of tissue paper. Danny does the same for Charlotte, only his backup flower is his friend Skipper dressed in a silly flower costume! The episode was hilarious, and it was just one of many where Demi really shined.

Demi's work on *As the Bell Rings* really prepared her for a serious television and movie career with the Disney Channel. It got Demi accustomed to the long hours of performing on a steady television show and also helped her improve her acting skills. But her role on *As the Bell Rings* also introduced Disney to Demi's music and amazing voice. One of Demi's original songs, "Shadow," was featured on an episode of *As the Bell Rings*. That must have meant a lot to Demi. Disney's vote of approval definitely gave her confidence in her music. The fans loved the song and Demi's voice!

Demi's developing television career may have been exhausting and demanding at times, but Demi handled it all with sophistication and a mature and professional attitude. She focused on getting her work done, but she also managed to have a lot of fun and make some amazing friends. Demi was finally securely on her way to stardom, and there was no looking back anymore for her.

CHAPTER 5:
This Is Me

Demi's roles on *Barney & Friends* and *As the Bell Rings* may have gotten her name out there, but it was her role as Mitchie Torres in the Disney Channel Original Movie *Camp Rock* that catapulted her into superstardom and made her the teen queen she is today.

In *Camp Rock*, Demi stars as Mitchie Torres, a girl who dreams of attending a summer camp for the performing arts called Camp Rock. Lots of Camp Rock alumni have made it big, including pop star Shane Gray, played by real-life music superstar, Joe Jonas. Shane is in a band called Connect 3. His band members are played by Joe Jonas's real life band members (and brothers!) Nick and Kevin Jonas. Mitchie has dreams of being discovered at Camp Rock for her amazing voice and songwriting skills. But money is tight in Mitchie's family and she doesn't think her parents can afford to send her to camp. But then Mitchie gets the surprise of her life when her parents tell her that they have figured out a way that allows her to go to the camp after all. Mitchie's mom landed a job as the camp cook, and with Mitchie's help in the kitchen, they can afford to send Mitchie to Camp Rock!

Soon enough, mom and daughter pack up their bags and drive to the camp. When Mitchie arrives at Camp Rock, she can tell immediately that there are tons of talented kids who will be camping with her. There are musicians, dancers, and, of course, some really big egos to deal with.

Mitchie is so worried about impressing her fellow campers that she finds herself lying to fit in. She tells everyone that her mom is the president of a television company, Hot Tunes TV China. This simple lie catches the attention of the biggest drama queen in camp, Tess Tyler. Tess has a famous mother, and considers herself to be the biggest star of Camp Rock. Tess hopes that Mitchie's mom can help Tess launch her career so she invites Mitchie to stay in her bunk along with her two friends, Ella and Peggy. In order to stay friends with Tess, Mitchie has to make sure her secret about her mom's real job stays safe.

After helping her mom in the morning, Mitchie attends classes during the day in dance, singing, and songwriting. It turns out that Shane Gray has returned to Camp Rock as a dance instructor after fighting with his bandmates. The other two members of Connect 3 think Shane needs to get rid of his bad attitude and get back to his roots — and Camp Rock is the perfect place to do that. Mitchie is so excited that one of her teachers is a true legend. Plus, he's totally cute. After finishing her kitchen duty on one of the first mornings, Mitchie plops down at an empty piano to work on one of her original songs. Shane Gray hears her and is completely captivated, but he doesn't see who she is. He spends his entire time at camp searching for the girl with the voice.

Mitchie and Shane end up hiding out in the same lakeside spot a few times and slowly become friends. They have a lot in common, and they both really enjoy each other's company. But Mitchie has no idea he's searching for her and her song. Their growing friendship is obvious to Tess, who is totally jealous, since she, just like every other girl at Camp Rock, has a crush on cutie Shane. She starts digging to find something she can use against Mitchie to get Shane's attention for herself and discovers the truth about Mitchie's mother.

After Shane and his band perform a rockin' concert, Tess figures it's the perfect time to get her revenge. She tells a crowd of campers, including Shane, that Mitchie has been lying about her mom's job, and that she's actually the camp cook, not the president of some big foreign television corporation. Shane can't believe that Mitchie lied to him, especially since he trusted her more than anyone else at Camp Rock. He feels like Mitchie has really let him down.

Mitchie thinks her final chance to redeem herself in Shane's eyes is at the camp's Final Jam. Too bad Tess is one step ahead of her and plants her expensive one-of-a-kind charm bracelet so it looks like Mitchie stole it. The camp director finds out about Mitchie's supposed burglary and bans her from participating in any camp activities until after Final Jam. Mitchie is totally bummed, but she's smart enough to find a way around the situation.

Final Jam goes on with some really awesome performances. Then the camp director announces it is the conclusion and Mitchie begs him to let her go onstage. Since Final Jam is technically over, he allows her to perform. Mitchie gathers her courage and bravely performs her song "This Is Me." Shane, who is watching the performance, recognizes her voice as the one he has been searching for all summer. Shane then joins Mitchie on stage, filled with excitement about finally finding that perfect voice. "This Is Me" turns into a duet with Shane and Mitchie rocking out to the awesome song, made even better by the best singers in Camp Rock!

Believe it or not, Demi had no idea who was playing her love interest in *Camp Rock* when she booked the part. "I actually didn't even have any idea that the Jonas Brothers were going to be in the movie until after I got it," Demi told *Access Hollywood*. Imagine Demi's surprise when she found out she would be starring in a movie with one of the hottest teen bands ever! The Jonas Brothers are all adorable and Demi was already a huge fan, so having Joe Jonas as her costar was a big honor.

Demi had previous experience working on television shows, but she had never been the main character in a feature movie. Demi filmed at multiple locations, which meant she traveled a lot. They filmed at several different summer camps in Canada and on soundstages in Los Angeles. That combined with working long days on set, must have been exhausting. But she got through it all with energy to spare.

Demi had the honor of singing the first song of *Camp Rock* called "This Is Me," which set the tone for the rest of the movie. "This Is Me" would also be a song featured at the end of the movie. Demi told *Access Hollywood*, "You can either focus on being scared of the pressure and tons of cameras or you could look at it as, 'Well if you didn't want it, then why have you been practicing in your bedroom on Friday nights when you had the choice to go out?'" Demi had a lot of work ahead of her to learn all of her lines, lyrics, and choreography, but luckily she had a whole cast full of new friends to help her out, including the super cute Jonas Brothers! And they were definitely used to that kind of stress.

Even though she was super excited to be filming the movie, Demi was probably still nervous to star in a movie with the Jonas Brothers. To add to her nervousness, she would have to share some pretty romantic scenes with Joe. But she didn't have to worry, because the Jonas Brothers are true to their reputation as sweet, respectable guys. "*Camp Rock* was awesome! They're awesome guys and they're very classy," Demi told *Access Hollywood*. That's not what most people expect from rock stars. Even though Nick and Kevin weren't in the movie as much as Joe, the brothers and their parents were often on the set of the movie and spent a lot of time with Demi.

Demi's stepdad, Eddie, was also on the set of the movie. He has served as Demi's manager for many years and was right there to support and help her every step of the way. The filming schedule was very hectic, and Demi put a lot of pressure on herself to be perfect in every scene. But Eddie was great at helping Demi calm down when she was being too hard on herself. Demi told *The Houston Press,* "I need him in the mornings and at night and for support." "Some days it gets so stressful that I can be in tears. *Camp Rock* was my first movie, and in the first two weeks, I got really sick of exhaustion. I was in my trailer sweating. Drips of sweat were just coming off me because I was so stressed. It really does affect your health — how much you work, especially being this young . . . But you get used to it." After a couple of weeks, Demi was able to relax into her role and enjoy the rest of the filming.

Demi's journey was very similar to her character Mitchie's journey in *Camp Rock* — minus the whole part about lying about her identity! Like Mitchie, Demi truly had her dream come true by being discovered for her talent and getting a chance to perform alongside a music superstar. Demi couldn't believe her dreams were coming true. She told *Access Hollywood*, "Even though I was at the *Camp Rock* premiere, and my face is on the poster, it still didn't hit me that like, I felt like screaming myself, 'cause I was so excited!"

Demi used insight about how she acted while she was in school to develop her character in *Camp Rock*. "Throughout the movie, [Mitchie] learns more about who she is and becomes more confident. Standing out instead of trying to fit in," Demi told *The Houston Chronicle*. "That was the kind of thing that I was going through in middle school, just being able to accept who I was. Once I did, everything got a lot easier." Demi's life experiences really helped bring Mitchie to life for viewers. "I wish I would have focused more on my schoolwork, rather than being popular. I think Mitchie should have done that, too — just focused on having a good time at camp rather than being popular. It ends badly if you're trying to impress someone," Demi told *J-14* magazine.

Although Demi did get to play a beautiful girl with a rockin' voice who gets the guy of her dreams, Demi had some not-so-graceful moments during filming too. Like having her face covered in flour, and falling with a twelve-pound bag of potato chips that spilled every-where, including in her hair. What a mess! Demi told Shine On Media, "One day I had to throw flour in my face and I looked horrible." But at the same time, Demi did have some glamorous moments, like sharing a lot of screentime with total hottie Joe Jonas.

In the end, Disney and Demi had created something totally unique and appealing to viewers. *Variety* reports that 8.9 million viewers tuned into the premiere of *Camp Rock*. On Friday, June 20, 2008, the day of the premiere, everything changed for Demi. She went from a somewhat well known teen working to achieve her dreams to a household name. Eventually, *Camp Rock*

would reach 35 million U.S. viewers as reported by *Entertainment Weekly.*

What really blew Demi away was the amount of extra stuff that comes along with starring in a Disney movie — like doing interviews, photo shoots, and all of the products put out for fans to buy. "I was looking through the product book before anything came out, and there was a lawn chair and a lamp. I was like, 'All right, whatever,'" Demi told *The Houston Chronicle.* Demi's face on a lawn chair and a lamp, and even pillowcases? She certainly hadn't expected that!

Camp Rock was so successful that Disney decided to do a sequel. Demi has confirmed that she will be returning to play the role of Mitchie Torres. Demi told *Entertainment Weekly*, "I'm not even sure what it's going to be about, I swear! I know as much as you do!" No matter what it's about, you can bet it's going to be totally awesome — especially since Demi and the Jonas Brothers will be the stars!

CHAPTER 6:
Just the Jonas Brothers

One of the best things about working with the Jonas Brothers on *Camp Rock* wasn't the movie itself for Demi. It was the friendship she formed with the three talented brothers. Demi has a lot in common with Joe, Nick, and Kevin — especially when it comes to music. She loves writing her own songs, and so do they. The four of them had lots of impromptu jam sessions on set and they had a great time making music together. So when Hollywood Records signed Demi to their label, she turned to the Jonas Brothers to help her with her debut album. Kevin, Joe, and Nick are also signed to Hollywood Records and were more than happy to work with Demi. They helped her write and even produced some of her songs! Demi recorded her first album very quickly, but then had to wait all summer before it would hit store shelves.

Of course Demi had no plans to sit around on her couch waiting for her album to come out. Instead, she was going on tour with the Jonas Brothers! In 2008, Demi was the opening act for the Jonas Brothers on their "Burnin' Up" North American tour. Demi must have been really nervous to open up for one of the hottest bands in America. She knew the Jo Bros loved her music — but what about their fans? Would they be into Demi's sound? To help calm her nerves, Demi did the only thing she could do to prepare — practice, practice, and more practice!

Demi performed several smaller concerts to prepare before hitting the road for the main event. "It's taught me how to stay intact with the audience and not panic, how to handle mistakes and things like that.

I've dropped the microphone several times," Demi told *The Houston Chronicle*. That's not to say that she didn't have her share of mistakes on stage during really big shows, but all the practice certainly helped her learn how to handle them!

Demi's biggest worry was her self-professed clumsiness. She's quick to warn people that she's a total klutz, so she was really worried about tripping, falling, and dropping things while onstage. "I'm very uncoordinated," Demi revealed in an interview with *People* magazine. "I'm surprised I don't fall onstage more." Of course, even with lots of practices, mistakes happen, especially when on a different stage with a different layout every night. "I fell at a show this one time," Demi told *MTV News*. "Actually, I've fallen several times — like, four times already. But this one time I fell, it was the only one that made Perez Hilton and YouTube. I didn't think anything of it when it happened. I just laughed it off onstage. But the next day, I see that it hit the Internet, and I was like, 'Nooooooo.' It totally stung, because I wasn't expecting it." The media was quick to poke fun at Demi for her fall, but she just shook it off with a little help from the Jonas Brothers. "But I didn't get hurt, and Joe [Jonas] helped me out a lot with that. He made a ton of jokes about it," Demi explained to *MTV News*. Performance mishaps can certainly be embarrassing, but it's great that Demi learned to handle them gracefully pretty early on in her career.

On June 18, 2008, Demi performed her first warm-up concert at the Palace Theatre in Syracuse, New York. She went on to perform at several Six Flags locations, including ones in Upper Marlboro, Maryland; Chicago, Illinois; Springfield, Massachusetts; and Jackson, New Jersey. She also tried out her performance skills at the House of Blues in New Orleans and Cleveland. Demi finished off her mini-tour at New York City's Blender Theatre at Gramercy on June 28, 2008. After learning the ropes of performing, she was totally ready for the screaming fans that would be singing along at the sold-out Jonas Brothers performances.

Between *Camp Rock* coming out and the start of the "Burnin' Up" tour, Demi didn't get much of a vacation. In fact, her "vacation" was more like a few days of downtime. But Demi didn't mind. She was just eager to get out on the road and win over as many fans as possible. The "Burnin' Up" tour kicked off on July 4, 2008, in Toronto, Canada, at the Molson Amphitheatre to a packed house. Demi may have been nervous, but she totally got the crowd warmed up with her thirty-minute set.

During the fifth performance of the concert tour, Demi had a surreal experience. She was playing the Super Pages Arena in Dallas, Texas, near her hometown. It's one of Dallas's biggest arenas and Demi had actually gone to concerts there when she was growing up. "I was at a concert . . . at the stage I'm playing today, and I was watching Kelly Clarkson, and now I get to be up there, so it feels really great," Demi told NBC 5 News. Kelly Clarkson is one of Demi's idols, so performing on the same stage that Kelly had was a big moment for Demi.

Demi had a lot of other big moments on the road that summer — like celebrating her sweet sixteenth birthday. Most girls would have died for the chance to spend their birthdays with the Jonas Brothers, but it was just another work day for Demi. There was no way she was going to take a day off from performing, even to celebrate her birthday! She told *McClatchy Newspapers*, "On the day of my birthday, I had a concert, so 18,000–20,000 people were singing happy birthday to me. It was awesome." She also reported, "I celebrated it all day with my band and the Jonas Brothers." Demi didn't need a fancy party or a new car, a packed concert full of her fans was celebration enough for her. Demi told

Shine On Media, "The next night I had my party at Applebees with my band." That might seem pretty low-key for the newest tween sensation, but it fit Demi perfectly.

Even though a lot of the fans were primarily going to see the Jonas Brothers, Demi got her fair share of her own fans at the shows, especially after opening up for the Jo Bros multiple times during the tour. Demi told *MTV News* about the excitement of being on stage and living her dream. "The best part is the very second that I run out onstage after they say, 'Ladies and gentlemen, Demi Lovato,' I run out and people scream. It's surreal, because I go to concerts and I'm the one screaming, and [now] they're excited for me. It's just a great feeling." Demi got to experience that incredible feeling more than fifty times while touring with the Jonas Brothers. Another great feeling? Filming several shows for the Jonas Brothers: The 3-D Concert

Experience, a special 3-D concert movie! The movie hit the big screen on February 27, 2009, and gave Demi and Jonas Brothers fans the chance to see just what life is like on tour. Filming was super fun and Demi was psyched to give fans an inside look at life backstage!

Even though Demi rarely gets stage fright, she still sometimes gets just a little bit nervous before a performance. She even has a special trick that she uses to get rid of the jitters before she goes onstage, as she explained to *Seventeen* magazine, "To get over it, I do something a friend taught me: You look in the mirror and say, 'I am beautifully and wonderfully made.' Then you repeat it, each time emphasizing a different word. It makes you look at yourself in a whole different way." If that trick doesn't work, Demi can always turn to her supportive family to talk her through the nerves, and of course her best friend Selena is always just a phone call away for an encouraging pep talk!

Kevin, Joe, and Nick were great about encouraging Demi too. They've been incredible friends to her and they think of her as the little sister they never had — which can occasionally be a bad thing! Like when they pull pranks on her. Demi told Kidzworld.com all about the tricks up the Jonas's sleeves. "Oh yeah! There's a microphone on the side of the stage that we use to tell people if we need water or we need something, and it's called a talkback mike. Only we, the performers, can hear it in our earpieces. And there are times when the Jonas Brothers will use the mike to try to mess me up while I'm singing. There's been a few times that I've laughed in the middle of a song!" But in the end, it's all fun and games, and Demi probably pulled a few pranks on the Jo Bros too.

But, all kidding aside, the Jonas Brothers have really helped Demi adjust to her new life as a superstar. Going from an average small-town girl with a dream, to a famous face recognized everywhere can be quite an adjustment, and one that's not all that easy to make. So the help of Kevin, Joe, and Nick, was invaluable to Demi, as she told *McClatchy Newspapers*. "They taught me to stay anonymous in some places I go. They've just helped a lot on tour." Of course, Demi's friendship with the Jonas Brothers didn't end when the "Burnin' Up" tour was over. Demi told TV Guide Online, "they came to support me because they had the day off. And on their day off they came to my show. Which was just awesome, it felt great. And they're really great guys . . . what you see is what you get." The guys could have taken the day off to catch up on their sleep, but their friendship with Demi was much more important. What sweet guys!

With the "Burnin' Up" tour under her belt, Demi knew what it felt like to be a true music star. She loved everything about being tour, but one of the biggest highlights for her was performing in Texas. Demi told

The Dallas Morning News, "It gets hot in Texas, but I like it. Dallas, Texas, is absolutely my favorite city to perform in." Demi will definitely hit up her home state any time she gets the chance to perform there. Wouldn't you, if you were a superstar? Imagine all your old neighbors and classmates cheering you on! Demi loved Dallas best, but the show that really made her feel like a star was in New York City. "There was like three days in a row when we played Madison Square Garden and nothing can top that. It's just like it's legendary and it felt awesome to be there," Demi told Shine On Media. Madison Square Garden is one of the most famous concert venues in the country — and Demi got to play it on her first tour! She knew what a big deal it was and treasured every single moment. Hopefully, it was only the first of many times she'll play there and the first of many tours. "I know how excited I get when I go see concerts and people that I love. And I know every song of theirs. So to know that there are people in the audience that are excited to see me, it's still surreal. And I hope it never changes. I hope I never get used to it," Demi told TV Guide Online. She might not want to get used to giving concerts, but her fans could definitely get used to having Demi perform in their towns!

CHAPTER 7:
Don't Forget

After several months on tour, it was finally time for Demi's first album, *Don't Forget*, to release in September 2008. So why did Demi choose that name for the album? She told Shine On Media, "One of the songs in the album was really, really personal for me and it happens to be almost everybody's favorite and it's called 'Don't Forget,' so what better title to have for your first album, *Don't Forget*?" It's definitely an easy title to remember!

Demi's label, Hollywood Records, also represents a lot of Demi's fellow Disney stars like the Jonas Brothers, Miley Cyrus, the Cheetah Girls, Hilary Duff, and Vanessa

Hudgens, just to name a few. But they also rep the Plain White Tees, Hayden Panettiere, and Jesse McCartney. Although she has representation from an excellent and very well-known record company, Demi really pulls her own weight by being an incredibly talented performer, and by constantly working to improve her talent and expand her range of work. Not only does Demi have a powerful voice, but she's also a great songwriter. In fact, Demi wrote a lot of the songs on her album. It was very important for Demi to record as much of her own music as she could, since she feels that her songs are a big part of who she is. Songwriting is the best form of therapy that Demi knows. When she has a bad day, she dives right into writing exactly what she's feeling, and before she knows it, she's in a much better mood and she has a killer new tune!

Since Demi uses songwriting to get out her feelings, most of her songs come straight from her own experiences and whatever happens to be going on in her life. "Whenever I write music, it's never planned. I'm always either playing guitar or piano first, and then I'll write lyrics to it. But I love writing lyrics about experiences I've had in my life," Demi told Kidzworld.com. In fact, part of the reason that so many fans relate to Demi is that she sings about things that have really happened to her, which makes her music feel honest and real. Plus, lots of kids can relate to the types of things that Demi has gone though — from falling in love to dealing with mean girls to getting dumped. Demi told Shine On Media that her favorite song is . . . "I guess I like 'Middle.' Because I guess it kind of showcases the notes I can hit and stuff like that. I had a lot of fun recording that 'cause I was like going all out on that song."

Some of Demi's songs probably surprised her fans. The songs she sang for *Camp Rock* were very upbeat pop songs, but Demi likes a little more rock in the music she writes. Demi told *The Houston Chronicle*, "People have definitely said they weren't expecting the album to be as rock as it is. They were expecting the butterfly pop stuff." Not to say that there is anything wrong with "butterfly pop stuff," it just isn't the type of music that Demi is into. Demi has been through some rough times, and she has never been afraid to write about being sad or down. Demi told *MTV News*, "I used to write [really dark] songs every night in my room — like, five or six a night — and I'd be up until five in the morning, and my mom would come up and say, 'So what are you writing?' I'd play her a song, and she'd go, 'Wow — go to therapy.' But it really is therapy for me so I put everything in my lyrics." Demi and Hollywood Records worked together to pick the songs for her debut album, and they left most of the darker songs off, but that doesn't mean fans won't get to hear them eventually. "You won't necessarily find a lot of that on the album, but hopefully you will on the next album. It's my first one, so I wanted it to be fun — stuff you can drive around in your car to and jam out to," Demi told *MTV News*.

Demi loves all types of music — from jazz to R&B to pop — but her all-time favorite is rock. Her favorite band is the pop punk group Paramore, whose lead singer, Hayley Williams, is also Demi's fashion icon. But Demi's love for rock music doesn't end there. Demi's a fan of AC/DC, The Devil Wears Prada, and the heavy metal band Job for a Cowboy. "[Metal isn't] all I listen to, of course, but there was a period of time where it was," Demi told *MTV News*. "I guess it started in school. I started listening to stuff with screaming in it, and then I started [exploring] more metal. MySpace helped me a lot, and friends will tell me about certain bands. And some of the bands I like aren't necessarily too metal. It's funny, because the Jonas Brothers dance and play dance music in their dressing room, and I'll be across the hall, and I just blare metal. People walk by and go, 'Really?'" A few people might be surprised by Demi's diverse tastes, but she knows that exploring different genres of music only makes her own music stronger and more unique, since she borrows a little bit from everything she likes! She might snag a drum beat from a hiphop song and mix it with jazzy lyrics and a rock and roll guitar line. The result? Pure Demi!

Although Demi really likes rock, she definitely looks up to pop stars like Kelly Clarkson, Christina Aguilera, and Hilary Duff too. Demi told *MTV News* that she really admires Hilary Duff's ability to balance her private life with her public personna. Demi told *MTV News*, "[She] has stayed a really good role model." "I mean, I'm sure she made mistakes, but you never saw them. I think it's really cool that someone can grow up and continue to be looked up to by young girls." Demi really cares about her fans and being a good role model for them, just like Hilary Duff. And Demi has always been inspired by Kelly Clarkson, as she told

DEMI
LOVES
ROCKIN' OUT!

Tim Mosenfelder/Getty Images

Demi
ROCKING
on her guitar.

Jon Kopaloff/FilmMagic/Getty Images

Demi at the L.A. premiere of *Twilight*.

Demi goes **GLAM** at the 2008 MTV Video Music Awards.

Demi poses with country singer Taylor Swift at the American Music Awards.

**Demi performing
in front of
THOUSANDS
of fans.**

Demi at the New York *Camp Rock* premiere.

Demi with fellow Disney stars Miley Cyrus and Selena Gomez at the 2008 Teen Choice Awards.

Kevin Mazur/WireImage/Getty Images

The Jonas Brothers, Alyson Stoner, and Demi at the European premiere of *Camp Rock.*

Entertainment Weekly, "Kelly Clarkson, when she first went rock, was totally my inspiration. I decided to try it and it was like, 'Wow, this fits more.'" Kelly will always be one of Demi's favorite singers. She only hopes that she can be just as inspiring to other young girls and introduce them to a little bit of rock and roll.

Demi wrote a lot of the songs on her album, but she also got help from the Jonas Brothers and other popular musicians. "I tend to write songs that are, I guess, a little bit more intense and less catchy, and I needed help writing catchy songs," she admitted to *MTV News*. "I did a duet with the Jonas Brothers on my album, and we wrote the song together." "It's like a breakup song, and it's called 'On the Line.' [It was important to have them on my album] because, I mean, just look at how successful they are. I would love to have their input anytime, because they're obviously doing something right." With their well-loved pop songs, the Jonas Brothers definitely know a lot about successful music, and they also know that Demi's sound has that special something that makes her stand out from the crowd. "We're really proud of her," Nick Jonas told *Access Hollywood*. "She's got an amazing voice and working with her in the studio was also a lot of fun."

So what was it like to be working with the Jonas Brothers in a music studio instead of on the set of *Camp Rock*? Demi told Shine On Media, "it was more creative . . . It's kind of like learning a choreographed dance as opposed to freestyling . . . movies you already have a script and you already know what you're going to do and you kind of just go in and do your job, but in the studio it's all off the top of your head and it's all creative work." Along with the Jonas Brothers' participation on the album, there is also a song that features Robert Schwartzman, who is the front man for Rooney, an all-guy band that puts out some really great and catchy songs. "So that's where they came in. I put a lot of my musical input and lyrics into these songs, and they just helped me with hooks and stuff like that," Demi told *MTV News.*

Demi may have had some help perfecting her songs, but the album is still very, very personal. Demi told *MTV News,* "There's a song I wrote myself that I hope fans will react to and connect with. The song is about feeling insecure and just not feeling pretty, and I hope girls my age can relate to it, because I just felt like there needed to be a song about how not everyone has confidence. I know it sounds cheesy, but it's true." Demi definitely inspires a lot of confidence in her fans. She is proof that you can reach your dreams by being absolutely true to yourself, and not trying to be someone you aren't.

Finally, on September 23, 2008, Demi's album hit store shelves. Demi told *McLatchy Newspapers,* "It's awesome. It's crazy. I can't believe I'm actually coming out with an album. I'm very nervous, but I'm excited at the same time." Demi must have been extra excited when she found out that her album made #2 on the *Billboard* charts. Demi told Shine On Media that she found out the day she appeared on *Ellen*. She said, "I was at my house and I was getting ready to leave for the studio and my dad came in and told me." At first, she said, "It didn't process in my mind." But, after it sunk in Demi was totally excited and screaming for joy!

After listening to *Don't Forget*, it's hard to believe that Demi recorded the entire album in ten days! And it definitely wasn't easy. Demi told Shine On Media that the most difficult part about the recording process was that: "We had ten days to record the entire album . . . Within those ten days we got a lot done, but it was very, very long days and it was very difficult." If *Don't Forget* is what Demi can do in only 10 days, imagine what she could do with a few weeks in the recording studio!

Putting out an album is more than songwriting, touring, and recording music in a studio. It also involves making one or more music videos. Demi was already a pro at singing on film, so she was really excited to film the music videos for *Don't Forget*. Demi recently told *MTV News*, "I just shot a video for 'Get Back,' and it turned out awesome. Hopefully, we'll do that with more of the songs, and hopefully, you'll like them." Demi also shot a music video for her song, "La La Land." Demi told Shine On Media, "It was my first crazy, long day video. It was awesome, though." Demi's fans definitely thought it was awesome too!

With the release of her new album, Demi did several special performances. The one that made Demi's family especially proud was when Demi sang the national anthem at the Thanksgiving Day Dallas Cowboys football game on November 27, 2008. It was an extra special performance for Demi's mom since all the Cowboys fans that she used to entertain were now watching her daughter, brave and talented, singing by herself while surrounded by thousands of people.

Even though Demi was excited, she was a little shaken up before her live performance, for good reason! She said in an interview with Shine On Media, "I was extremely nervous. I don't think I've ever been that nervous in my life . . . In rehearsal a bee came by and like flew by my face. So I was like, OK, so I'm either gonna trip and fall again or there's a bee that's gonna sting me in the face like while I'm singing that national anthem." Luckily, there were no bees in sight when she was singing live. Demi made her family so proud with her flawless performance!

As for future albums, Demi would like to continue doing collaborations. "I hope to do a collaboration with Kelly Clarkson," she said. "She's done collaborations with Reba McEntire, who was her idol growing up, and Kelly Clarkson has been my idol growing up. Hopefully, one day I could collaborate with her — that would be the biggest dream come true." Demi is only sixteen and most of her dreams have already come true, so it probably won't be long before she adds that one to the list too! She's already working on songs for her sophomore album, so keep a look out — it will be in a store near you before you know it!

CHAPTER 8:
True Princesses

Selena and Demi's friendship kept them close long after *Barney & Friends* ended, but they haven't been involved in the same movie or television show since then. While Demi filmed *As the Bell Rings* and *Camp Rock*, Selena starred in the hit Disney Channel series *Wizards of Waverly Place*. Both girls have been super successful, but they each secretly hoped they would get the chance to share the screen again. Luckily, Disney had the same idea.

The creative folks at Disney got together and decided to make a Disney Channel original made-for-television movie just for Demi and Selena. The result was *Princess*

Protection Program. When Demi and Selena found out that they were going to be in the same movie they were ecstatic! Both girls have such crazy schedules between recording music and acting, so they were really excited to finally get to spend a lot of time together. Plus, they'd get to hang around by the beach and travel to Puerto Rico, where the movie was being filmed!

In *Princess Protection Program*, Demi plays Princess Rosalina and Selena plays Carter. When an evil dictator wants to take over Princess Rosalina's country she is spirited away and put into the Princess Protection Program. The Princess Protection Program is an international agency that protects princesses who may be in danger. Princess Rosalina is hidden by a Princess Protection Program agent, Mason, at his home. He happens to have a daughter named Carter who is Rosalina's age. The only problem is the girls are total opposites. But Princess Rosalina has to hide her true royal identity, so, with Carter's help, she learns how to act like a normal teen. And Rosalina helps Carter too, by teaching her how to be more friendly and feminine to help get the attention of her crush, played by cutie Robert Adamson.

Even with the crushes and the comedy, *Princess Protection Program* has some serious drama. Demi told Shine On Media, "Its kind of more dramatic, I think, than people expect." Demi even had to shed a few tears! "I had to do like one or two serious crying scenes," Demi told Shine On Media. For example, she continues, "The first scene that I really have lines in I'm like bawling in a helicopter, being taken away from my family. It's pretty intense. I think it also has its really funny moments. So I guess you'd call it a dramedy."

Filming with Selena was an awesome experience for Demi. So great, in fact, that it was almost unbelievable. Demi told *Teen Magazine*, "Almost every scene we did, Selena would say, 'Oh my gosh, we're shooting a movie right now!'" Selena had filmed a couple of *Wizards of Waverly Place* specials that were as long as movies and Demi had filmed *Camp Rock*, but they were both still pretty new to the movie scene. Learning new tricks and getting into the swing of movie making was even cooler for both girls since they got to do it together.

Unlike in real life, Demi and Selena played two girls who do not get along because they can't accept each other's differences. Demi's character is a princess and Selena's character is more of a tomboy. Demi told Kidd Kraddick, "We fit our characters pretty well. Like even though I do a lot of rock music I'm still into makeup and I'm still an old pageant girl, so pageants mean a lot to me." As for Selena being similar to the character of Carter, Demi said "She's like a total tomboy, she wakes up in the morning and, like, eats nachos in, like, her basketball shorts." Demi and Selena, unlike their characters, knew right away when they met that opposites can attract! Selena has always been more of a tomboy than Demi, and Demi has always been more into girly things. But the two girls have a lot in common too.

Selena had a similar childhood to Demi. She was raised in Grand Prairie, Texas, right near Demi. And Selena is a Disney darling as well. In *Wizards of Waverly Place*, Selena plays the main character Alex Russo, who lives on Waverly Place in New York City. Alex is different than most teenage girls because she has magical skills that she inherited from her parents. Alex and her two brothers, one older and one younger, have to compete with each other, magic trick by magic trick, because only one of them can keep their magical powers when they've grown up. The one who uses their magic in the best ways wins. Talk about sibling rivalry!

Selena isn't just a television star — she's also been featured on the big screen. She lent her voice to the film adaptation of *Horton Hears a Who!* alongside big Hollywood names like Steve Carell, Jim Carrey, Isla

Fisher, and Jesse McCartney. Selena voiced all of the mayor's daughters in the movie. She told the *New York Daily News*, "I had to change up my voice to do higher voices, and then bring it down to do lower voices. All of the mayor's daughters look different, so I play many different characters." Selena also starred as Mary Santiago in *Another Cinderella Story*, a great story about a girl overcoming the odds to pursue her dream of dancing. Selena also sang a few songs on *Another Cinderella Story*'s soundtrack. She sang "Tell Me Something I Don't Know" and a duet called "New Classic" with total hottie Drew Seeley.

Demi and Selena have been there for each other every step of the way from their very first roles to good and bad auditions to small parts and rejections and then on to the big roles that have made them stars. Sharing all of that, good and bad, has made their friendship incredibly strong. Demi told *Teen Magazine*, "And then it just hits us! We've been working at this for a really, really long time. We met each other the day we started working on [our careers], so it's pretty ironic how things turn out. It's been awesome." Now the twosome can enjoy their success and celebrate it together, which makes it all even sweeter! Finally getting the chance to work together and share the screen again was just icing on the cake for Demi and Selena!

So what was filming a movie with her best friend actually like? It was better than Demi could have ever imagined! Selena told *Teen Magazine*, "The most glamorous [aspects of my job] would have to be hair, makeup, and wardrobe. I really couldn't get up and do my hair like this or my makeup or get all of these nice clothes." Demi and Selena got to get their makeup done together, get fitted in wardrobe, and share all the awesome clothes! Selena's wardrobe included lots of shorts and T-shirts, which was just fine with her, but Demi got to wear a few really fun and frilly princess dresses. The food on set was pretty awesome too. Both

Demi and Selena love to eat, so they probably spent lots of down time at craft services! Demi told *Cosmogirl*, "When me and Selena were taping [*Princess Protection Program*] in Puerto Rico, they had a lot of fried foods. So all I ate was beans and rice! And ice cream!" There were probably a lot of sleepovers too!

But, it wasn't just Demi and Selena time, all the time. Selena told *TWIST*, "The cast is close. When we were done shooting, we'd hang out at the pool or go to dinner." Selena also told *TWIST*, "We also went surfing!" Both Demi and Selena were really bummed when filming finished. They were having too much fun for it to be over so quickly! But the cast got to reunite to do press for the release of *Princess Protection Program* and definitely still keep in touch.

Of course the best part of filming a movie is getting to see how the fans like it. "Me and Selena are totally stoked for it to come out," Demi told Shine On Media. Their fans were stoked too — the movie was a total hit! The experience was so amazing that Demi and Selena would definitely love to film another movie together again, and their fans would love it too. So, who knows, there may be a *Princess Protection Program 2* in the future!

CHAPTER 9:
Demi Takes a Chance

Demi was bummed after filming for *Princess Protection Program* wrapped. She had had such an amazing time working in Puerto Rico with Selena that it was probably a little disappointing to go back to her normal life. But it wasn't long before Demi had a new adventure to look forward to. She would be filming her very own TV show called *Sonny With a Chance* on the Disney Channel. *Sonny With a Chance* was Demi's biggest job yet, as she would not just be filming a TV show, but she would also have the extra responsibilities that come along with being the main character. Unlike in a movie, the star of a television show develops her character over many episodes, so there is a lot more time to get into the role. Demi knew she had a lot of work in front of her, but she was psyched. Demi loves a challenge and she was ready to take the next step in her career.

Before the Disney Channel settled on the title *Sonny With a Chance*, they bounced around some other potential names. At times the show was called, *Welcome to Molliwood*, or just plain *Molliwood*, but eventually the Disney executives settled on the really unique title, *Sonny With a Chance*. Demi described the basic premise of *Sonny With a Chance* to MTV News, "The show is actually a sitcom. It's the Disney version of *30 Rock*, . . . On that show, we have a rivalry with another show, and there's so many, like, crazy plot lines. I play this girl who comes to L.A., or Hollywood, and is kind of thrown into all this madness." *30 Rock* is a really popular show on NBC. In 2008 alone, in its fourth season, *30 Rock* won the Golden Globe for Best

Comedy, Best Actress (Tina Fey), and Best Actor (Alec Baldwin). With Demi on board, *Sonny With a Chance* is sure to be up for some awards after it's first season too!

On the show, Demi plays Sonny, a Midwestern girl who just landed a job on her favorite television show, *So Random.* "I play Sonny, who's a girl from Wisconsin, and she kinda sticks out like a sore thumb, 'cause she's very quirky and very over the top," Demi told *MTV News.* "And she's, like, this little Midwestern or Wisconsin girl I kind of can relate to." Specifically, Demi told *MTV News* that the real similarity between herself and Sonny is that "I'm from Texas and I'm thrown into this [thing that's like], 'Whoa everything is awesome.' It's really interesting." With the impressive acting skills Demi showed off when she played Mitchie in *Camp Rock*, she totally makes Sonny her own!

Aside from her acting experience, Demi has a talented supporting cast who are quirky and funny in their own rights. The cast includes budding actress Tiffany Thornton as Tawni Hart. Tawni is the diva of *So Random*. Tiffany has a good amount of experience when it comes to acting on television shows and in movies. She has guest starred in shows like *Hannah Montana, Wizards of Waverly Place, The O.C.,* and *That's So Raven*. Most recently, she filmed a Disney Channel original made-for-television movie called *Hatching Pete* with *Hannah Montana* cutie Mitchel Musso and *Minutemen* star Jason Dolley. Brandon Smith is another one of Demi's co-stars on *Sonny with a Chance*. Brandon plays Nico Harris, a smooth comedian. Brandon was also on the Disney Channel, appearing in shows like *That's So Raven* and *Phil of the Future*.

Demi's love interest on *Sonny With a Chance* is played by super cute actor Sterling Knight. Sterling stars with *High School Musical* hottie Zac Efron in the movie *17 Again*. Sterling also appeared on *Hannah Montana*

as Lucas in the episode "My Best Friend's Boyfriend." So, with such a cute co-star, has Demi seen any chemistry off set? Demi told TeenHollywood.com, "Sterling is awesome. He's one of my closest friends and we actually argue a lot like our characters do but it's because we have such a great friendship." It looks like Demi and Sterling might just be good friends, at least for now!

The cast of *Sonny With a Chance* starred with Demi in another project before the first episode of the show ever aired. They joined Demi in the music video for her hit song "La-La Land". Demi told Shine On Media, "In one scene Tiffany is playing your stereotypical diva walking down the street with shopping bags . . . Brandon plays like a photographer . . . each one has their own different scenario." Even though she was working with and surrounded by a lot of her friends while filming the "La-La Land" music video, Demi said it was still a lot of hard work. "It was my first crazy long day video. It was awesome though," Demi told Shine On Media.

Of course, even though filming a television show is hard work, the process isn't always serious business. During downtime, Demi and the cast found plenty of time for snacking, talking, goofing off, and playing pranks on each other. Demi admitted to Shine On Media, that when fellow castmate Tiffany Thornton and Demi aren't in a scene, sometimes they will "Stick our hands like through the doorway so you can see our fingers. Kind of like only things that you would know if you watched for it." The pranks didn't stop there. Demi told TeenHollywood.com, "One time, we had a food fight scene in the cafeteria at the commissary and they had these bread rolls and bagels and we were waiting to go into the scene. We had rolls and we were like, 'I wonder if they will ever notice if we roll a bread roll across the set?' They did." Don't worry, Demi didn't get into *too* much trouble!

Aside from pulling pranks, Demi has also gotten to do some crazy stuff on set. Especially because *Sonny With a Chance* is a comedy about a show within a show, things can get a little wacky. Demi described one episode to Shine On Media, "There was one where I got to dress up like a boy and that was pretty interesting." Demi also admitted to Shine On Media, "I wore a fat suit which was also pretty interesting." Demi has also been spotted on the set covered in ketchup and dressed up like a bee!

But Demi's experience as the lead in a television show hasn't been all Hollywood glamour. Just like her not-so-pretty moments in *Camp Rock*, Demi had her share of funny moments while filming *Sonny with a Chance*. In one episode, she told TV Guide Online, "I started off really nervous and in the first take I messed up all the words. Overall, though, it turned out very well." As for her messiest moment? Demi told TeenHollywood.com, "I guess the ones that involve food. Like you have to continue, throughout the day, with egg salad all over you. I broke out with an allergic reaction and that was challenging. It splattered onto me and I got blotchy and everything." Luckily, Demi's reaction eventually went away, but she definitely won't be having egg salad anytime soon!

One thing about her new show that has Demi especially excited is the prospect of having her friends guest star. Demi has confirmed that Selena Gomez will be making at least one appearance on *Sonny With a Chance.* Demi told TeenHollywood.com, "We kind of played rivals in [the Disney Channel movie] *Princess Protection Program* so I'd like to do a role where we play friends. She will be guest-starring. She shoots with us in a couple of weeks." Selena is totally excited about being on *Sonny With a Chance.* Selena told *MTV News,* "We'd love to have Demi on ['Wizards.'] And I'd love to be a guest star on her show." So far, no confirmations have been made as to if the Jonas

Brothers will be making an appearance on *Sonny with a Chance*, but there's always hope!

Demi was probably pretty nervous before her show debuted, but she had nothing to worry about. *Sonny With a Chance* premiered with the most viewers for it's time slot from kids ages 6-14. And it was the most watched show on cable that night! Pretty soon everyone is going to know Demi's name, and she couldn't be more excited about it!

CHAPTER 10:
Behind the Scenes

When she isn't filming, recording, or touring, Demi enjoys just relaxing and taking a few minutes to be a normal teenager. She loves hanging out with her family and friends, and jumps at any chance to do that. Her schedule is so hectic that breaks aren't guaranteed, but she always looks forward to the holidays because she knows she'll get a chance to see her family then. Even when she's taking time off, Demi loves writing music. Demi is a fairly laid-back girl. So when she has time to herself she likes to go shopping, catch up with her friends, listen to music, and hang out at home instead of going to parties.

Demi's family is the most important part of her life and her biggest support system. Her mom, stepdad, and sisters have moved with her to Los Angeles since commuting from Dallas was pretty stressful for everyone. So Demi gets to see them every day. But, as Demi grew up, maintaining a relationship with her father, Patrick, became very important to her. They got to talk on the phone and e-mail, but their visits were few and far between. Demi had been too young to travel on her own before, but after not seeing her dad for four years, Demi missed him a lot. So in 2008, she decided it was time to take a trip and go see her dad. Patrick was staying at Demi's grandfather's house in New Mexico. Demi and her father were finally able to enjoy a brief but heartwarming reunion. Her father was so surprised to see Demi at his front door! But when the shock of seeing his daughter for the first time in four long years wore off, all he could think about was how beautiful she looked, and how much he had missed her.

Patrick supports his daughters no matter how far away they are. He watched *Camp Rock* in his home in New Mexico. He told *Star Magazine*, "'I thought she did a wonderful job," he says. "It was so exciting for me to see my little girl, and so emotional too." Hopefully the two will be in touch more often now, despite Demi's overwhelming schedule. And now, whenever he wants to see Demi but can't because of the distance or because he isn't feeling good enough to travel, all Patrick has to do is turn on his television and tune into the Disney Channel!

In January of 2008, Demi's stepdad, Eddie, quit his job as a manager at a Ford dealership in Texas so he could focus entirely on being Demi's manager. It is important to Eddie that Demi maintains her strong family values in spite of her fame. Eddie told *The Washington Post*, "We said when this all started that we'd keep our family values, and that's what we're doing." Eddie travels with Demi to her many auditions and her tour locations to cheer her on before she steps on the stage. He is very supportive of Demi's career choices and always looks out for her best interests. Eddie is always a parent first and a manager second. So he's not about to let Demi do anything for her career that he feels is inappropriate for her personally or that isn't OK for a girl her age. Like when Demi was doing a photo shoot for the magazine *J-14*, she asked her stepfather if she could dye her hair black. At first he said "No!" But in the end he did let Demi dye her hair, but only one shade darker than her natural hair color. Did you know that Demi still has a curfew, even when she's on tour? That's right, Eddie makes sure she's either back in her hotel room or back at her house by midnight every night, no matter what! Even when he's not with her on the road, he calls her hotel room until she answers, and he's sure she is safe!

Even though it may sound like Eddie is a pretty strict dad, he just wants what is best for Demi. After all, she still is a teenager. Demi told *The Washington Post,* "We have a lot of trust in each other." Both of Demi's parents want her to be happy, healthy, and safe at all times. Demi's mom will always be Demi's biggest fan. She is so proud of the success Demi has already achieved and she is also really happy that Demi has stayed true to who she is. Dianna told *Tiger Beat,* "I keep expecting one day I'm going to wake up and she's going to be different, but she's not. She's the same kid she's always been. I tell her to go for it with everything she's got!" Demi's parents know that they raised her well and can trust that Demi will always make good decisions for herself.

Another great support system for Demi are her friends. Demi told *GL Magazine,* "My best friend Marissa came out to be my 'assistant' last summer on tour, but it was really just an excuse for her to stay in my room and hang out every night and spend weeks together," Demi told *GL.* The girls had a lot of fun that summer, especially hanging out with the Jonas Brothers. The girls got to travel all around the country together. "She's always been the one person who I could go to with any problems," Demi told *GL Magazine*. Marissa and Demi have been friends for a really long time and hopefully will get to keep spending a lot of time together despite Demi's crazy schedule!

When Demi needs to talk to someone about the stresses of being the star of a television show, or just how to deal with fame in general, she definitely turns to her other best friend Selena. Demi and Selena love living a life of fame and fortune, but they also enjoy being silly and just having fun like other teenagers. Demi said on Kidzworld.com, "We always find the most random fun. When we were eight or nine, we'd always use accents wherever we went. Once, we went into Target on the Fourth of July, and we were speaking in British accents asking everyone why they were wearing red, white, and blue." Some things don't change, no matter how famous Demi gets — and her friendship with Selena is one of them! In fact, the girls "totally act like kids when we're around each other. We don't worry about trying to fit in. We have a good time," Demi told *The Cleveland Plain Dealer.*

In an interview with *Teen Magazine*, Selena opened up about her amazing friendship with Demi. She said, "I think that it's so nice to go through all of this with someone that I love and that I care about and that I can trust. Because we're sixteen-year-old girls dealing with things, like being afraid to go outside [because of the paparazzi] . . . Our lives have changed since I've known her since I was seven. It's just nice to have that support because it's very hard to come out to L.A., we're both from Texas, and not know anybody and not be able to trust anybody." Demi and Selena are always there to support each other in the good times and bad, just like best friends should be.

108

Not only do Demi and Selena spend a ton of ti
together, but they also share clothes — even on the red
carpet! Demi told *J-14*, "At my first premiere that I went
to with her, Selena was wearing all my clothes. We
always borrow each other's jeans, and we have
Converse and switch them up by accident." It must be
nice to be the same size as your best friend! As for her
own fashion style, Demi likes to dress with a little bit of
an edge. As she explained to *The Fit for MySpace.com*,
"My personal style is kind of sophisticated edgy I guess.
I wear a lot of black and I guess it's just what I feel
comfortable in." She loves the colors black, white, and
red and is a total accessories junky. Demi told *The Fit
for MySpace.com*, "I'm a huge accessories person. I
love chunky jewelry, but lots of like rhinestones. I grew
up in pageants so anything glitzy is fine by me."
Sometimes she wears 80's style clothing including leg
warmers and pastel shirts. Demi also loves

ute tights with a dress. She definitely knows
polish off her looks with the right mix of fun and
n!

But even fashionable stars like Selena and Demi have days where they don't feel as pretty as they are. One of the best things about their friendship is that they help boost each other's self esteem on bad hair days. Selena told *J-14*, "Demi's the kind of person who is honest with me, and there to support me and tell me, 'Don't listen to that. Know who you are.' And that really means a lot to me. . . ." And Selena does the same for Demi! They are each other's biggest cheerleaders. "I think the toughest thing for me is being able to tell myself that I'm beautiful. Selena totally helped me through growing up and dealing with a changing figure and face. She's always been there," Demi told *J-14*. When Demi gets the blues, Selena is the one that she can always turn to. And vice versa. Demi revealed in a *Seventeen* magazine interview, "I can totally go to

[Selena] with any problem and she will not judge me, no matter what. I've gone to other friends before and said, 'Hey, I really like this guy,' and they've been like, 'Really? *Him*?' But Selena would always say, 'If you're happy, go for it!' I can trust her with anything, and she can trust me — we'll definitely take each other's secrets to the grave." Trust is such a major factor in any friendship, and it looks like Selena and Demi have more than enough of it to be BFF's for life!

Even though Demi and Selena spend a lot of time together, they don't just hang out with each other. The girls have developed friendships with lots of the fellow actors and performers in L.A. They love hanging out with the Jonas Brothers, and both girls spend a lot of time with Jennifer Stone, who is one of Selena's costars on *Wizards of Waverly Place*. And guess what? Jennifer was born in Texas too! No wonder Demi and Selena like her so much!

When Demi and Selena want to reach out to their

fans, they do it over the Internet. In January 2008, they decided to start posting videos on YouTube for their fans, featuring their fun and sometimes-hilarious conversations, tours of their hotel rooms, and updates on their busy, exciting lives. These videos have each been viewed over a million times! It was the perfect way for both girls to keep in touch with their fans, since they couldn't possibly answer every e-mail and message from fans personally. "Selena and I were noticing how hard it can be to write messages and comments to every single fan that you have. On YouTube, even though you're not speaking to them personally, you can at least say, 'Hey, this is what I'm doing,' and you're getting to reach out to all of them. So, we made a video and all of a sudden it became this huge thing that other people were doing, too," Demi told Kidzworld.com. Lots of other stars post YouTube videos now as well, including Miley Cyrus and her friend Mandy, and the Jonas Brothers. Miley and Mandy even posted a silly video pretending to be Selena and Demi. Some people thought the video was mean, but Selena and Demi thought it was funny!

Being a star means that Demi has to be careful not to let gossip and rumors get out of hand. Miley and Mandy's YouTube video sparked lots of rumors that the stars don't get along, but that's not the case at all. They've actually become friends, since they both work for Disney and go to lots of the same events. Demi went to Miley's sixteenth birthday party, and Miley told *Popstar!* magazine, "We were just, like, having fun. . . . They have, like, a YouTube account, and so at the end of our video we did put 'Go to their YouTube.' . . . We were kind of supporting their channel, but also being silly because they were being funny, and that's our thing — to be funny. . . . Elvis says, 'Imitation is the greatest form of flattery,' so we were imitating them being funny." Selena Gomez told *Tiger Beat*, "The feud is just a rumor," and Demi chimed in, "There's no rivalry between us." Another rumor that Demi had to handle? That she was dating one of the Jonas Brothers. Demi told *Entertainment Weekly*, "Joe and I never dated. We're really good friends. I just think it's funny that people try to pin me to them. It's like, 'Oh, come on!' I think [if I were going to] I would have dated one of them by now!"

Demi may not have dated a Jo Bro but she did have a brief romance with another Disney Channel hottie, Cody Linley. Demi and Cody originally met when Demi was taking acting lessons from Cody's mom, Cathryn Sullivan. Cody told *Blast Magazine*, "We had a romance scene together in acting class and we had to kiss . . . Afterward we talked about it for hours. We were still just friends then, but it started to turn into something more. Now we're on hold because we're both so busy, touring, recording her album and filming another TV movie, so I won't get much chance to see her. I hope we can reconnect again, because she's a terrific girl and she's a lot of fun." With both of their hectic schedules the two did manage to find time to go on a date, but it didn't turn out too well. First, Cody's car broke down on his way to pick up Demi so he was two hours late. Then, Cody told *Seventeen* Magazine, "We went to a steak place for dinner. Demi's family actually let her stay out until eleven that night with me, even though she had to get up early for a five a.m. flight. So then we went to the grocery store and bought like toothpaste and tweezers and then I managed to get her home safely. I was really worried that my car was going to break down again, and then I got lost on my way home." Luckily, everyone got home safe, but Cody's car was another story. It had to get fixed the next day! Right now Demi isn't officially dating anyone but she hasn't totally written it off. Demi told *GL*, "Of course it's hard with scheduling or whatever, but if you like somebody you make it work."

Along with her family and friends Demi cares a lot about her fans. That's why Demi has made it one of her goals to teach her fans to treat everyone the way they would like to be treated — and no one wants to be picked on or bullied! Demi remembers how hard it was to feel confident and good about herself in middle school when so many people were bullying her. She hopes that speaking out about her experience can inspire other girls. "I guess the way that I want to impact girls as a . . . role model — it's not me not making mistakes because I'm going to make mistakes, but one day I want to help with bullying," Demi said on a visit to the *Ellen DeGeneres Show.* After all, Demi is living proof that anyone can get past bullying and go on to achieve their dreams.

Along with speaking out against bullying in interviews, Demi also uses her MySpace page to reach out to her fans and spread her message about the damaging effects of bullying. She wrote on her MySpace page, "As a message to everyone, please keep in mind when you're about to threaten someone or make fun of them or leave blog comments about them, that what you say or do can truly affect someone." She continued, "Cheesy and lame as it may sound, never forget the golden rule." These are definitely words everyone should live by! Unfortunately, bullying happens in every school and community — and even big stars like Demi aren't completely immune. She probably still has days where a negative review or a mean blog post about her or her music makes her feel bad. But Demi just stays strong and reminds herself of all the reasons she loves herself. She knows that no one can make you feel bad unless you let them — and Demi never lets anyone get to her for long!

Demi's life has changed dramatically over the past few years, and it will probably never be the same. But she's lucky to have her family and friends to keep her grounded, support her through the bad days, and celebrate with her on the good ones. But what really keeps Demi going is the belief she has in herself! She knows that she has the talent to succeed and that she has a lot to offer the world with her music and acting. Luckily, Demi's fans know it too! And none of us can wait to see what she accomplishes as her career really heats up!

CHAPTER 11:
Demi's Future

Demi has come a long way since that performance in her kindergarten talent show when she decided she wanted to sing. From her first episode on *Barney & Friends* to the last scene she filmed for *Sonny With a Chance*, Demi's life has changed so much!

Demi has her fingers crossed that there will be several more seasons of *Sonny With a Chance*, since she loves working on it so much. As she explained to TV Guide Online, "Each episode gets funnier and funnier. It's very crazy. I was nervous in the beginning. It's hard to carry a comedy show. If you're not funny, the show is not going to be funny. I've never had a lot of confidence in comedy, but I've really let loose and totally had fun with it." Demi may have been nervous, but she pulled herself together and delivered a stellar performance in every episode. Disney is super psyched about the show, so there is a good chance that there will be lots more *Sonny* in Demi's future!

With a show on Disney and a hot debut album, critics have been quick to compare Demi to fellow Disney star Miley Cyrus. Demi is totally flattered by the comparison, since she is a big Miley fan, but Demi told *MTV News*, "I am who I am. I'd like to be Demi Lovato. If I can accomplish half of what [*Miley's*] done, it'd be an honor, but I'd like to do it as Demi." Demi's fans can rest easy — Disney isn't trying to turn Demi into a clone of Miley. Quite the opposite! They know that Demi is special and unique and they want to showcase all the things that separate her from the pack. Which is just fine with Demi! "I've been doing what I've always been doing, which is not trying to live up to anybody else's expectations," Demi explained to *Teen Magazine*. Demi is going to be famous on her terms or not at all. So you'll never catch her taking a role just to please producers or changing her sound because her record label thinks it will boost her sales. Demi's music is part of who she is and, while her sound will change and grow as she gets older, it will always be true to who she is. And, in her acting career, Demi's only signing on to projects that she feels will challenge her as an actress and that will be inspirational and entertaining to her fans! For now, she's just taking it one day at a time and trying to make the best choices she can. "I'm not even thinking about five years. But hopefully I'll still be touring and doing my TV show; obviously I'll continue that. I want to start doing movies, like feature films. And I would love to maybe direct one day," Demi told *Entertainment Weekly.* Demi has set some big goals for herself, but considering what she's already accomplished in her teens, there is no doubt that she will achieve everything she's ever dreamed of!

Of course, Demi's biggest focus for her future is her music. She loves singing and songwriting more than anything else, and you can bet Demi will still be making music even if no one ever buys another one of her albums. Not that she has to worry about that! She's got a tour lined up for 2009 and is already hard at work on songs for her second album. Demi recorded her first album in just ten days, but she's taking a little more time with her next. She wants to include even more of her own original songs and she's hoping her fans will love them. So keep an eye out for Demi's sophomore album towards the end of 2009. You won't want to miss it.

No matter what, things are just getting warmed up for Demi. Need proof? In 2008, Demi was named one of the 10 Breakout Stars of 2008 by *Forbes Magazine*. It was a huge honor to be recognized for everything she had accomplished that year, especially considering the other big names that made the list! Demi shared this honor with celebrities including David Cooke, Robert Pattinson, Katy Perry, and some of her close friends, like the Jonas Brothers and Selena! Demi told *Forbes Magazine* about her philosophy for the future. "I just have to keep working and have fun. Having fun is the most important part." If the future is anything like the past few years for Demi, she'll be having fun working for a long, long time to come. Demi may have broken out in 2008, but she'll really be coming into her own in the next few years, so keep your eyes peeled for all the incredible things Demi has been working on!

CHAPTER 12:
Quiz: How well do you know Demi?
Take this quiz, and find out!

1. What is Demi Lovato's full name?

   a. Demetria Levonne Lovato

   b. Demi Devonne Lovato

   c. Demetria Devonne Lovato

   d. Devonne Demetria Lovato

2. What did Eddie DeLaGarza do for a living before becoming Demi's manager?

   a. Chef at a top-of-the-line Dallas restaurant

   b. Quarterback for the Dallas Cowboys

   c. Telemarketer for a phone company

   d. Car salesman

3. How did Demi meet her BFF Selena Gomez?

   a. At grade school

   b. At an audition for *Barney & Friends*

   c. At a playground near Demi's house

   d. At a Disney Channel casting call

4. What song did Demi perform at her kindergarten talent show?

   a. "My Heart Will Go On"

   b. "Twinkle, Twinkle, Little Star"

   c. "La-La Land"

   d. "The Star-Spangled Banner"

5. How did Demi meet the Jonas Brothers?

   a. They went to grade school together

   b. They starred together in *As the Bell Rings*

   c. They starred together in *Camp Rock*

   d. They starred on *Barney & Friends*

6. What did Demi's character Mitchie Torres lie about in *Camp Rock*?

    a. That she was a professional singer

    b. Her mother's real job as a chef at *Camp Rock*

    c. That she didn't like Shane Gray

    d. That she really did steal Tess's charm bracelet

7. What type of music is Demi's fave?

    a. Rap

    b. Bubblegum pop

    c. Classical

    d. Heavy metal

8. Which of the following is one of Demi's idols?

    a. Kelly Clarkson

    b. Madonna

    c. Beyoncé

    d. Miley Cyrus

9. What is the name of Demi's first album?

   a. *Please Forget*

   b. *Forget*

   c. *Don't Forget*

   d. *Can't Forget*

10. What are Demi's favorite colors?

   a. Yellow and orange

   b. Black, black, and more black!

   c. Red, black, and royal blue

   d. Pink and light blue

11. Which of the following is not a song on Demi's album, *Don't Forget*?

   a. "La La Land"

   b. "I Wish"

   c. "The Middle"

   d. "Don't Forget"

12. What jobs did Demi's mother, Dianna, have before Demi was born?

a. A Dallas Cowboys cheerleader, and country music recording artist

b. A violin player in the Dallas symphony, and a country music recording artist

c. A Dallas Cowboys cheerleader and a car saleswoman at the local Ford dealership

d. A trapeze artist in a circus, and a Dallas Cowboys cheerleader

13. Which one of Demi's original songs was featured on *As the Bell Rings*?

a. "La-La Land"

b. "Get Back"

c. "Shadow"

d. "Believe in Me"

14. Where was Demi's BFF Selena Gomez born?

a. Tokyo, Japan

b. Berlin, Germany

c. New York, New York

d. Dallas, Texas

15. How does Demi feel about Miley Cyrus?

a. She sees Miley as her competition

b. She is Miley's biggest fan

c. She feels like it's an honor to be compared to her, but that she is very different from Miley

d. She doesn't know who Miley Cyrus is

16. What was the name of the tour that Demi did with the Jonas Brothers?

a. The "On Fire" Tour

b. The "Burnin' Up" Tour

c. The "Raise the Roof" Tour

d. The "Three Brothers" Tour

17. Which of the following is one of Demi and Selena's favorite things to do together?

   a. Hanging out at rockin', super crowded, Hollywood parties

   b. Going to amusement parks and riding the Tilt-a-Whirl all day

   c. Scrapbooking and taking lots of pictures

   d. Staying in, watching a good movie, and having a sleepover

18. What is engraved on the inside of Demi's purity ring?

   a. "True Love Waits"

   b. "Wait for Love"

   c. "Love Will Come"

   d. "Give Love a Chance"

19. What are Demi's sisters' names?

   a. Austin and Dallas

   b. Madison and Lexington

c. Dallas and Madison

d. Madison and Devonne

20. How many times have Demi and Selena's YouTube videologs been viewed?

a. Over a thousand times each

b. Over a billion times each

c. Over a million times each

d. Over a hundred times each

ANSWER KEY:

1. C	11. B
2. D	12. A
3. B	13. C
4. A	14. C
5. C	15. C
6. B	16. B
7. D	17. D
8. A	18. A
9. C	19. C
10. C	20. C

If you correctly answered . . .

15-20 Questions: You're a Demi expert! Watch out Selena, Demi has a new BFF!

9-14 Questions: Not too shabby! You probably know all the lyrics to a few of Demi's songs, and you just might become one of Demi's biggest fans.

5-8 Questions: Almost there. You like Demi, but can't say you're a huge fan, yet. Maybe you should see Demi in concert, and you might become a bigger fan!

1-4 Questions: You just met Demi. This weekend, relax on your couch and catch up on some Demi greats: *Camp Rock*, *As the Bell Rings*, and *Princess Protection Program*. Then, plug in some of her best songs, and absorb all that is Demi!

CHAPTER 13:
Just the Facts

Full Name: Demetria Devonne Lovato

Birthday: August 20, 1992

Hometown: Colleyville, Texas

Parents: Diana and Patrick Lovato, stepdad Eddie DeLaGarza

Siblings: older sis, Dallas Lovato and younger sis, Madison DeLaGarza

Hair Color: Chocolate brown

Eye Color: Dark brown

Height: 5'2"

Best Friend: Selena Gomez

Celebrity Crushes: Jim Sturgess, and William Beckett from the band The Academy Is

First Acting Gig: *Barney and Friends*

Favorite Holiday: Christmas

Favorite Colors: red, black, and royal blue, and other dark colors.

Favorite Clothing Brands: Chloe and Burberry

Favorite Store: Forever21

Favorite Foods: pickles, cheese, eggs, Rice Krispy treats, tacos, and chocolate

Favorite Fruit: Oranges

Favorite Outfit: black sweater cardigan with a little red dress and black tights

Favorite Accessory: Funky hats

Favorite Movie: *Donnie Darko*

Favorite Power Ranger: Pink

Favorite Sport: surfing

Favorite Band: Paramore

Favorite Paramore song: "Born for This"

Other Favorite Music: Duffy, Kings of Leon, Biffy Clyro, Job for a Cowboy, AC/DC, Mötley Crüe, Devil Wears Prada, and of course the Jonas Brothers!

Most Embarrassing Moment: She was at the beach with the cast of *Wizards of Waverly Place*. She was in the ocean and a wave came and took her bikini top and while she was tying it back, another wave came and knocked off her bikini bottoms! At least Selena and Jennifer Stone were the only witnesses!

Must-Have Accessory: A purity ring, engraved with "True Love Waits," which she wears on a chain around her neck.

CHAPTER 14:
Demi Online

Demi is pretty busy these days between working on her television show, checking out movie scripts, touring, and, of course, penning songs for future albums, so her story is constantly changing. To keep up with all the latest Demi news, check these websites often! But always ask your parents' permission before getting online and be careful while surfing. Never give out any personal information, like your address or the name of your school, without checking with your parents first! And don't worry if your favorite website disappears one day. Websites come and go, so there is sure to be a new one to replace it soon.

http://www.demilovato.com/index.php

This is Demi's official website. It has the latest Demi news, photos, an online store, tour info, and much, much more. Add it to your Favorites so you never miss a Demi update!

www.myspace.com/demilovato

This is Demi's official MySpace page. You can find updates on Demi, listen to Demi's music, see photos, read Demi's blog, and leave Demi a message in the comments section. She checks it pretty regularly, so she's sure to read your words of encouragement and support!

http://tv.disney.go.com/disneychannel/originalmovies/camprock/

This is the official website for *Camp Rock*. It's packed with awesome extras like music videos, games, interviews with the campers, and even a store where you can order your own *Camp Rock* gear!

http://tv.disney.go.com/disneychannel/sonnywithachance/index.html

This is the official website for Demi's show *Sonny with a Chance*. It has all sorts of great stuff about the show like video clips, character biographies, fun downloads like wallpaper and icons, and games!

www.youtube.com/user/therealdemilovato

This is Demi and Selena's official YouTube channel. They post videos here of them doing funny things so they can connect directly with their fans — check it out for a good laugh, plus all the latest Demi and Selena info straight from the stars themselves.